Psalm Simple Prayers

Devotional book 3

DONNA ROBINSON

ISBN: 1537064444
ISBN-13: 978 1537064444

DEDICATION

I dedicate this book to all who search to understand the knowledge of our
Lord and Savior Jesus Christ.

CONTENTS

BOOK 3 OF 5 WRITTEN BY DAVID, ASAPH, HEMAN, ETHAN, & SONS OF KORAH

ACKNOWLEDGMENTS

I would like to acknowledge the Lord Jesus Christ for using me as a vessel of the Holy Spirit, the wisdom to write, the motivation to mature, and the patience to progress.

INTRODUCTION

As said in Book 1, I wrote this book in need of understanding why David was described as "A man after God's heart" (Acts. 13:22 & 1 Sam. 13:14). Unfolding the Psalms seek the truth of our need of His presence and purpose yesterday, today, and forevermore (Heb. 13:8).

Book 3 is one of the shorter books with strong meaning in understanding Old Testament covenant. Keep an open mind when reading these Psalms as you journey through biblical history.

THE PURPOSE OF THIS DEVOTIONAL BOOK:

1. **STUDY** THE PSALM
2. **READ** THE REVEALTION
3. **RELEASE** PRAYER

CONCEITED PLEASURES VS COMMITTED PURPOSE

Psalm 73
A psalm of Asaph.

1 Surely God is good to Israel,
  to those who are pure in heart.
2 But as for me, my feet had almost slipped;
  I had nearly lost my foothold.
3 For I envied the arrogant
  when I saw the prosperity of the wicked.
4 They have no struggles;
  their bodies are healthy and strong.
5 They are free from common human burdens;
  they are not plagued by human ills.
6 Therefore pride is their necklace;
  they clothe themselves with violence.
7 From their callous hearts comes iniquity;
  their evil imaginations have no limits.
8 They scoff, and speak with malice;
  with arrogance they threaten oppression.
9 Their mouths lay claim to heaven,
  and their tongues take possession of the earth.
10 Therefore their people turn to them
  and drink up waters in abundance.
11 They say, "How would God know?
  Does the Most High know anything?"
12 This is what the wicked are like
  always free of care, they go on amassing wealth.
13 Surely in vain I have kept my heart pure
  and have washed my hands in innocence.
14 All day long I have been afflicted,
  and every morning brings new punishments.
15 If I had spoken out like that,
  I would have betrayed your children.
16 When I tried to understand all this,
  it troubled me deeply
17 till I entered the sanctuary of God;
  then I understood their final destiny.
18 Surely you place them on slippery ground;

you cast them down to ruin.
19 How suddenly are they destroyed,
    completely swept away by terrors!
20 They are like a dream when one awakes;
    when you arise, Lord,
    you will despise them as fantasies.
21 When my heart was grieved
    and my spirit embittered,
22 I was senseless and ignorant;
    I was a brute beast before you.
23 Yet I am always with you;
    you hold me by my right hand.
24 You guide me with your counsel,
    and afterward you will take me into glory.
25 Whom have I in heaven but you?
    And earth has nothing I desire besides you.
26 My flesh and my heart may fail,
    but God is the strength of my heart
    and my portion forever.
27 Those who are far from you will perish;
    you destroy all who are unfaithful to you.
28 But as for me, it is good to be near God.
    I have made the Sovereign Lord my refuge;
    I will tell of all your deeds.

How easy it is to become envious and jealous of others and what they have. The root of these fleshly thoughts and desires must be cut off at the head by abstaining from the false pretensions of satisfaction. Asaph was dealing with the desires of the fast life, money, careless living, and fantasy realities with no rules to live or abide by. He wanted to understand the possession and delight of these things to the point of almost losing his mind! Then he realized the things that are unseen (supernatural) are more real than the things that are seen (natural) (vs.7).

Asaph entered into the rest of God for his purpose in life and its' meaning. Daily our flesh and feelings we hold cause us to be desperate for earthly matters and not spiritual encounters. Taking the high road will always advance us successfully without fail. Those who choose otherwise will fail with success passing them by.

PRAYER

Surely God You are good to me! You have always provided a way of escape for me (1 Corinth. 10:13) even when You knew I would choose otherwise. What is unseen by man is never unnoticed by You Oh God (2 Chronicles 16:9). Give me the strength to rid myself of vein intentions, relationships, morals, and character. As I take the high road hold me close with Your right hand (vs. 23) and guide me with Your counsel. I wash my life of the past and those who claim to know You from my life **NOW**! My purpose, identity, and my very next breath come from You. My flesh and my heart fails but God is the strength of my heart and my portion forever (vs. 26). It is good for me to draw near to God I have put my trust in the Lord God that I may declare all thy works (vs. 28) in Jesus name I pray Amen.

REMEMBER US

Psalm 74
A maskil of Asaph.

1 O God, why have you rejected us forever?
  Why does your anger smolder against the sheep of your pasture?
2 Remember the nation you purchased long ago,
    the people of your inheritance, whom you redeemed
    Mount Zion, where you dwelt.
3 Turn your steps toward these everlasting ruins,
    all this destruction the enemy has brought on the sanctuary.
4 Your foes roared in the place where you met with us;
    they set up their standards as signs.
5 They behaved like men wielding axes
    to cut through a thicket of trees.
6 They smashed all the carved paneling
    with their axes and hatchets.
7 They burned your sanctuary to the ground;
    they defiled the dwelling place of your Name.
8 They said in their hearts, "We will crush them completely!"
    They burned every place where God was worshiped in the land.
9 We are given no signs from God;
    no prophets are left,
    and none of us knows how long this will be.
10 How long will the enemy mock you, God?
    Will the foe revile your name forever?
11 Why do you hold back your hand, your right hand?
    Take it from the folds of your garment and destroy them!
12 But God is my King from long ago;
    he brings salvation on the earth.
13 It was you who split open the sea by your power;
    you broke the heads of the monster in the waters.
14 It was you who crushed the heads of Leviathan
    and gave it as food to the creatures of the desert.
15 It was you who opened up springs and streams;
    you dried up the ever-flowing rivers.
16 The day is yours, and yours also the night;
    you established the sun and moon.
17 It was you who set all the boundaries of the earth;
    you made both summer and winter.
18 Remember how the enemy has mocked you, Lord,
    how foolish people have reviled your name.

19 Do not hand over the life of your dove to wild beasts;
   do not forget the lives of your afflicted people forever.
20 Have regard for your covenant,
   because haunts of violence fill the dark places of the land.
21 Do not let the oppressed retreat in disgrace;
   may the poor and needy praise your name.
22 Rise up, O God, and defend your cause;
   remember how fools mock you all day long.
23 Do not ignore the clamor of your adversaries,
   the uproar of your enemies, which rises continually.

My focus on this Psalm is to consider the plea of restoration of the church; and the people of Israel as revenge on the enemies who have destroyed the temple and the land. The psalmist is unknown but is heartfelt about the present destruction throughout their sacred places of worship. Being careful to remember the covenant God made with them as a chosen people. The psalmist tested God with His own promise (vs. 20). Countless attacks against the church felt like a slow never ending battle; but the contrast of God's victories of old hold an outlasting ability of true redemption in this situation. Our first reaction to pressure from the enemy must be to speak what the word of God says about that situation and God will respond to His covenant keeping word.

PRAYER

Father you have given us a command that we shall have no other gods before You (Exo. 20:3). I honor Your New Testament covenant that permits the Holy Spirit to dwell in this temple (in me).

Any distraction, addictions, opposition, hindrances, blockage, or calamities that would come to destroy this temple (me) would be brought down to everlasting ruin. You no longer live in a box made from human hands (Exo. 25:10-22) but You live in our hearts (Eph. 3:17-19). Jehovah Nissi you will defend me as I set my praise toward You in the midst of this battle. I wage war against those battles with the words of Your covenant promise that says I am the righteousness of God through Christ (Rom. 3:21-24); and I am not forgotten in Jesus name I pray Amen.

GOD'S GREAT GAVEL

Psalm 75
For the director of music. To the tune of "Do Not Destroy." A psalm of Asaph. A song.

1 We praise you, God,
    we praise you, for your Name is near;
    people tell of your wonderful deeds.
2 You say, "I choose the appointed time;
    it is I who judge with equity.
3 When the earth and all its people quake,
    it is I who hold its pillars firm.
4 To the arrogant I say, 'Boast no more,'
    and to the wicked, 'Do not lift up your horns.
5 Do not lift your horns against heaven;
    do not speak so defiantly.'"
6 No one from the east or the west
    or from the desert can exalt themselves.
7 It is God who judges:
    He brings one down, he exalts another.
8 In the hand of the Lord is a cup
    full of foaming wine mixed with spices;
  he pours it out, and all the wicked of the earth
    drink it down to its very dregs.
9 As for me, I will declare this forever;
    I will sing praise to the God of Jacob,
10 who says, "I will cut off the horns of all the wicked,
    but the horns of the righteous will be lifted up."

Attention, Attention the gavel of righteousness and judgment are only for the Lord to handle! This is the main focus of this Psalm written by Asaph; but is inconclusive if it is about him or David. Either way God is appointed Judge in this Psalm of humility from the heart of a devout follower. No man should ever believe that he can esteem himself as a lone ranger and speak with a cocky dialogue. Promotion, advancement, harvest time, and appointed time are done by God alone. The Psalm points out "we" meaning every believer of God must give credit, honor, thanks and praise to the God in heaven who makes it all possible. The ending is a total surprise as it voices words from God speaking of the coming of an ultimate sacrifice for all who accept the great gavel of righteousness.

PRAYER

I praise You and give You thanks for not allowing man, my past, and my mistakes to dictate my judgment and how You see me. For promotion cometh neither from the east, west, nor from the south (vs. 6). God is the judge he putteth down one and setteth up another (vs. 7). My advancement comes from my kingdom obedience. I humble myself daily to the steadfastness of Your word that tells me right from wrong. You pour out Your cup of judgment on the just and the unjust. Let not lust of the flesh and pride of life (1 John 2:16) affect my decisions, family, purpose, attitude, reactions, thoughts, or my gifts. I give permission for Your gavel to focus my faith in Your promises for my life. In Jesus name I pray Amen.

OLD TESTAMENT VICTORIES

Psalm 76
For the director of music. With stringed instruments. A psalm of Asaph.
A song.

1 God is renowned in Judah;
   in Israel his name is great.
2 His tent is in Salem,
   his dwelling place in Zion.
3 There he broke the flashing arrows,
   the shields and the swords, the weapons of war.
4 You are radiant with light,
   more majestic than mountains rich with game.
5 The valiant lie plundered,
   they sleep their last sleep;
   not one of the warriors
   can lift his hands.
6 At your rebuke, God of Jacob,
   both horse and chariot lie still.
7 It is you alone who are to be feared.
   Who can stand before you when you are angry?
8 From heaven you pronounced judgment,
   and the land feared and was quiet
9 when you, God, rose up to judge,
   to save all the afflicted of the land.
10 Surely your wrath against mankind brings you praise,
   and the survivors of your wrath are restrained.
11 Make vows to the Lord your God and fulfill them;
   let all the neighboring lands
   bring gifts to the One to be feared.
12 He breaks the spirit of rulers;
   he is feared by the kings of the earth.

This Psalm is penned with great honor to God from Asaph about an awesome testimony of triumph. References of this Psalm are referred to only a certain battle in the Old Testament but this is not my particular focus. The revelation I take from this Psalm is how one must find victory in God in certain "places" in their life. Keywords: Judah (praise), Israel (covenant), Salem (peace), and Zion (city of David) indicate the "places" where He dwells in that time.

God's hand called attention to every believer and nonbeliever throughout the earth to be heard and witnessed as one to be feared (obeyed). The people committed themselves to these "places" in God and He filled their voices they made in Him. When we humble ourselves in these "places" and give our battles over to God He casts destruction on the very enemy out to attack you.

PRAYER

Victory is mine, victory is mine, victory today is mine! I take rest in the peace of God from the confusion of the enemy. I take rest in God as my praise will sound off in the ear of God for my restitution! I take rest in God for His everlasting covenant of the blood that renews me with strength. I make Zion the home of my heart where God dwells. Victory is mine, victory is mine, victory today is mine in Jesus name I pray Amen.

MIND GAMES

Psalm 77
For the director of music. For Jeduthun. Of Asaph. A psalm.

1 I cried out to God for help;
  I cried out to God to hear me.
2 When I was in distress, I sought the Lord;
  at night I stretched out untiring hands,
  and I would not be comforted.
3 I remembered you, God, and I groaned;
  I meditated, and my spirit grew faint.
4 You kept my eyes from closing;
  I was too troubled to speak.
5 I thought about the former days,
  the years of long ago;
6 I remembered my songs in the night.
  My heart meditated and my spirit asked:
7 "Will the Lord reject forever?
  Will he never show his favor again?
8 Has his unfailing love vanished forever?
  Has his promise failed for all time?
9 Has God forgotten to be merciful?
  Has he in anger withheld his compassion?"
10 Then I thought, "To this I will appeal:
  the years when the Most High stretched out his right hand.
11 I will remember the deeds of the Lord;
  yes, I will remember your miracles of long ago.
12 I will consider all your works
  and meditate on all your mighty deeds."
13 Your ways, God, are holy.
  What god is as great as our God?
14 You are the God who performs miracles;
  you display your power among the peoples.
15 With your mighty arm you redeemed your people,
  the descendants of Jacob and Joseph.
16 The waters saw you, God,
  the waters saw you and writhed;
  the very depths were convulsed.
17 The clouds poured down water,
  the heavens resounded with thunder;
  your arrows flashed back and forth.

18 Your thunder was heard in the whirlwind,
   your lightning lit up the world;
   the earth trembled and quaked.
19 Your path led through the sea,
   your way through the mighty waters,
   though your footprints were not seen.
20 You led your people like a flock
   by the hand of Moses and Aaron.

Wrestling with defeated thoughts of fear, faithlessness, insecurity, rejection, hurt, sadness, and weak emotions Asaph was about to lose it! He continuously uses the words thought and remembered. This intimidates his mind and projects his actions, atmospheres, and his reactions to occurring and recurring situations happening in his life.

I can familiarize myself in this Psalm crying out to God (vs.1). Praying until I had no words left (vs. 2) thinking more on my problems than the problem solver (vs. 3-6). Lastly agonizing on how deep the pain from those problems and feelings of being left all alone (vs. 7-9). At the brink of termination God steps into your situation and gives you a vision of His glory and promise over your life (vs. 10:12). Asaph declares who is greater than God (vs. 13)? He allowed the peace of God to rule in his mind as he knew that better days were ahead of him.

PRAYER

Today I clothe myself with Your armor the helmet of salvation to cover my mind (Eph. 6:17). This helmet protects me from the enemies blow. It gives me assurance of Christ reign in my life. Thank You for this helmet that connects me to the peace of the Mind Regulator to produce thoughts of supernatural substance to my situation. No longer will I involve myself with disquieted thoughts of defeat. I will cry out to God in faith that the core of my mind belongs to the Lord. The Lord will strengthen me with the words to produce spiritual weapons of war. I go in headfirst with my hands up into the deep where I find You, in Jesus name I pray Amen.

DISOBEDIENCE COST OBEDIENCE PAYS

Psalm 78
A maskil of Asaph.

1 My people, hear my teaching;
   listen to the words of my mouth.
2 I will open my mouth with a parable;
   I will utter hidden things, things from of old
3 things we have heard and known,
   things our ancestors have told us.
4 We will not hide them from their descendants;
   we will tell the next generation
  the praiseworthy deeds of the Lord,
   his power, and the wonders he has done.
5 He decreed statutes for Jacob
   and established the law in Israel,
   which he commanded our ancestors
   to teach their children,
6 so the next generation would know them,
   even the children yet to be born,
   and they in turn would tell their children.
7 Then they would put their trust in God
   and would not forget his deeds
   but would keep his commands.
8 They would not be like their ancestors
   a stubborn and rebellious generation,
   whose hearts were not loyal to God,
   whose spirits were not faithful to him.
9 The men of Ephraim, though armed with bows,
   turned back on the day of battle;
10 they did not keep God's covenant
   and refused to live by his law.
11 They forgot what he had done,
   the wonders he had shown them.
12 He did miracles in the sight of their ancestors
   in the land of Egypt, in the region of Zoan.
13 He divided the sea and led them through;
   he made the water stand up like a wall.
14 He guided them with the cloud by day
   and with light from the fire all night.

15 He split the rocks in the wilderness
    and gave them water as abundant as the seas;
16 he brought streams out of a rocky crag
    and made water flow down like rivers.
17 But they continued to sin against him,
    rebelling in the wilderness against the Most High.
18 They willfully put God to the test
    by demanding the food they craved.
19 They spoke against God;
    they said, "Can God really
    spread a table in the wilderness?
20 True, he struck the rock,
    and water gushed out,
    streams flowed abundantly,
    but can he also give us bread?
    Can he supply meat for his people?"
21 When the Lord heard them, he was furious;
    his fire broke out against Jacob,
    and his wrath rose against Israel,
22 for they did not believe in God
    or trust in his deliverance.
23 Yet he gave a command to the skies above
    and opened the doors of the heavens;
24 he rained down manna for the people to eat,
    he gave them the grain of heaven.
25 Human beings ate the bread of angels;
    he sent them all the food they could eat.
26 He let loose the east wind from the heavens
    and by his power made the south wind blow.
27 He rained meat down on them like dust,
    birds like sand on the seashore.
28 He made them come down inside their camp,
    all around their tents.
29 They ate till they were gorged
    he had given them what they craved.
30 But before they turned from what they craved,
    even while the food was still in their mouths,
31 God's anger rose against them;
    he put to death the sturdiest among them,
    cutting down the young men of Israel.
32 In spite of all this, they kept on sinning;
    in spite of his wonders, they did not believe.
33 So he ended their days in futility

and their years in terror.
34 Whenever God slew them, they would seek him;
   they eagerly turned to him again.
35 They remembered that God was their Rock,
   that God Most High was their Redeemer.
36 But then they would flatter him with their mouths,
   lying to him with their tongues;
37 their hearts were not loyal to him,
   they were not faithful to his covenant.
38 Yet he was merciful;
   he forgave their iniquities
   and did not destroy them.
   Time after time he restrained his anger
   and did not stir up his full wrath.
39 He remembered that they were but flesh,
   a passing breeze that does not return.
40 How often they rebelled against him in the wilderness
   and grieved him in the wasteland!
41 Again and again they put God to the test;
   they vexed the Holy One of Israel.
42 They did not remember his power
   the day he redeemed them from the oppressor,
43 the day he displayed his signs in Egypt,
   his wonders in the region of Zoan.
44 He turned their river into blood;
   they could not drink from their streams.
45 He sent swarms of flies that devoured them,
   and frogs that devastated them.
46 He gave their crops to the grasshopper,
   their produce to the locust.
47 He destroyed their vines with hail
   and their sycamore-figs with sleet.
48 He gave over their cattle to the hail,
   their livestock to bolts of lightning.
49 He unleashed against them his hot anger,
   his wrath, indignation and hostility
   a band of destroying angels.
50 He prepared a path for his anger;
   he did not spare them from death
   but gave them over to the plague.
51 He struck down all the firstborn of Egypt,
   the firstfruits of manhood in the tents of Ham.
52 But he brought his people out like a flock;

he led them like sheep through the wilderness.
53 He guided them safely, so they were unafraid;
    but the sea engulfed their enemies.
54 And so he brought them to the border of his holy land,
    to the hill country his right hand had taken.
55 He drove out nations before them
    and allotted their lands to them as an inheritance;
    he settled the tribes of Israel in their homes.
56 But they put God to the test
    and rebelled against the Most High;
    they did not keep his statutes.
57 Like their ancestors they were disloyal and faithless,
    as unreliable as a faulty bow.
58 They angered him with their high places;
    they aroused his jealousy with their idols.
59 When God heard them, he was furious;
    he rejected Israel completely.
60 He abandoned the tabernacle of Shiloh,
    the tent he had set up among humans.
61 He sent the ark of his might into captivity,
    his splendor into the hands of the enemy.
62 He gave his people over to the sword;
    he was furious with his inheritance.
63 Fire consumed their young men,
    and their young women had no wedding songs;
64 their priests were put to the sword,
    and their widows could not weep.
65 Then the Lord awoke as from sleep,
    as a warrior wakes from the stupor of wine.
66 He beat back his enemies;
    he put them to everlasting shame.
67 Then he rejected the tents of Joseph,
    he did not choose the tribe of Ephraim;
68 but he chose the tribe of Judah,
    Mount Zion, which he loved.
69 He built his sanctuary like the heights,
    like the earth that he established forever.
70 He chose David his servant
    and took him from the sheep pens;
71 from tending the sheep he brought him
    to be the shepherd of his people Jacob,
    of Israel his inheritance.

72 And David shepherded them with integrity of heart;
with skillful hands he led them.

The children of Israel were extremely a rebellion, impatient, ungrateful, and disobedient people. Asaph could not stand to see the next generation fall like this one. Relentlessly he made his mission to involve himself as a spokesperson to the people not to act in this way towards God. He instructed them with truth of God's miracles, His wrath, and His sustaining presence to a people that did not keep His commandments and begin to focus their hearts toward Him.

The wrath of God grew really heavy from disobedience as they chose the works of the flesh and not the works of God. They did not take Him seriously; so God moved on to an atmosphere and a willing vessel (David) who would accept Him. Asaph and David embodied in taking on the nature of God's love and His character. These men of God boldly accepted the task no matter the opposition, wilderness situation, or graven image set before them.

PRAYER

I call you a gracious Father today even when my heart was turned from You; the love of Your grace kept me alive. Forgive me of complaining, provoking the flesh, eluding false hope from human ability, and slick motives to have a place in my life. You called us to be and make disciples (Matt. 28:19); and be a witness of the word to all we know. You called us to be the salt of the earth (Matt. 5:13).

You called us to be set apart for Your glory (Rom. 1:1). I desire to be a representation to this generation as a world changer for Christ. I want to be a vessel; someone You can count on and trust to get Your job done. I receive the work of Your hands in my life **NOW**, in Jesus name I pray Amen.

CHURCH PRAYER

Psalm 79
A psalm of Asaph.

1 O God, the nations have invaded your inheritance;
    they have defiled your holy temple,
    they have reduced Jerusalem to rubble.
2 They have left the dead bodies of your servants
    as food for the birds of the sky,
    the flesh of your own people for the animals of the wild.
3 They have poured out blood like water
    all around Jerusalem,
    and there is no one to bury the dead.
4 We are objects of contempt to our neighbors,
    of scorn and derision to those around us.
5 How long, Lord? Will you be angry forever?
    How long will your jealousy burn like fire?
6 Pour out your wrath on the nations
    that do not acknowledge you,
  on the kingdoms
    that do not call on your name;
7 for they have devoured Jacob
    and devastated his homeland.
8 Do not hold against us the sins of past generations;
    may your mercy come quickly to meet us,
    for we are in desperate need.
9 Help us, God our Savior,
    for the glory of your name;
  deliver us and forgive our sins
    for your name's sake.
10 Why should the nations say,
    "Where is their God?"
    Before our eyes, make known among the nations
    that you avenge the outpoured blood of your servants.
11 May the groans of the prisoners come before you;
    with your strong arm preserve those condemned to die.
12 Pay back into the laps of our neighbors seven times
    the contempt they have hurled at you, Lord.
13 Then we your people, the sheep of your pasture,
    will praise you forever;
    from generation to generation

we will proclaim your praise.

An invasion of the church (temple in Jerusalem) has devastated the people of Israel. The "Ites" have come and wreaked havoc on their property of worship. Asaph pleads his case in prayer for the people of the nation to be forgiven, protected, delivered, strengthened, and comforted in this time of need (vs. 9). This temple was the sacred place where God resided and was acknowledged. This is the place where the people gave glory of His covenant instruction. In an instant some of the people of Israel were killed (vs. 2-3), some discredited of their beliefs (vs. 4), many condemned by the sins of the past (vs. 8), some imprisoned in innocence (vs. 11), and all rejected by people (vs. 10) with the feelings of abandonment as their condition in life.

Asaph prayed for restoration in the church and the glory of God's name to arise again from this horrible experience. This prayer recounts the dependence we should have in the rest of God, while in the midst of ridicule as a body of believers.

PRAYER

Lord you have called us to be fitly joined together as a body for your kingdom work (Eph. 4:16). I lift my church (your church name) up before You now as the bride of Christ (Eph. 5:27). I cover my Pastors, Ministers, Deacons (ness), and Elders of the church in the grace and blood of Jesus. I cover every youth, single father and mother, and widow in the grace and blood of Jesus.

I cover every ministry represented here at (name your church). Cover our worship, every seed sown, cover the parking lot to the front doors in the grace and blood of Jesus. Now Father cover the church body as a whole with Your word … no weapon formed against us will prosper (Isa. 54:17). Our faith and belief in Your word may be tested and tried but will never fail us. Now may the Lord be gracious to us and keep us make His face shine upon us and give us peace (Num. 6 24-26), in Jesus name I pray Amen.

RESTORE YOUR SHINE

Psalm 80
For the director of music. To the tune of "The Lilies of the Covenant."
of Asaph. A psalm.

1 Hear us, Shepherd of Israel,
   you who lead Joseph like a flock.
  You who sit enthroned between the cherubim,
   shine forth
 2 before Ephraim, Benjamin and Manasseh.
  Awaken your might;
   come and save us.
3 Restore us, O God;
   make your face shine on us,
   that we may be saved.
4 How long, Lord God Almighty,
   will your anger smolder
   against the prayers of your people?
5 You have fed them with the bread of tears;
   you have made them drink tears by the bowlful.
6 You have made us an object of derision to our neighbors,
   and our enemies mock us.
7 Restore us, God Almighty;
   make your face shine on us,
   that we may be saved.
8 You transplanted a vine from Egypt;
   you drove out the nations and planted it.
9 You cleared the ground for it,
   and it took root and filled the land.
10 The mountains were covered with its shade,
   the mighty cedars with its branches.
11 Its branches reached as far as the Sea,
   its shoots as far as the River.
12 Why have you broken down its walls
   so that all who pass by pick its grapes?
13 Boars from the forest ravage it,
   and insects from the fields feed on it.
14 Return to us, God Almighty!
   Look down from heaven and see!
   Watch over this vine,
15 the root your right hand has planted,

the son you have raised up for yourself.
16 Your vine is cut down, it is burned with fire;
  at your rebuke your people perish.
17 Let your hand rest on the man at your right hand,
  the son of man you have raised up for yourself.
18 Then we will not turn away from you;
  revive us, and we will call on your name.
19 Restore us, Lord God Almighty;
  make your face shine on us,
  that we may be saved.

Asaph continues his plea for the people of Israel to be restored in inheritance as God's chosen nation. The tenacity of his prayers were fierce with demands of stated testimonies of past experiences of God's hand at work in that nation. Tears, despair, gloomy, and dull appearance affected them every day. The nation of Israel remembered the beauty of God's covenant presence in their lives, land, and temple. Three times the plea for "restoration" and "shine upon us" was voiced in strong hopes that God would in fact do it for them again. Its' mention is so fervent that it describes parallel to the natural king at the present time and the King of Kings (vs.17) who would be soon to come.

PRAYER

Lord you are faithful in all of Your ways. I give You praise of Your wondrous works towards me that sometimes I don't even deserve. Help me to not allow the challenges of living a holy Christian life cause me to turn away from You. Even outside ungodly influences that attempt to hinder me. I pray You would cause Your face to shine upon me.

Every influence that has cost me consequences I pray You would restore me from the inside out. I am your masterpiece created for a purpose (Eph. 2:10), destined for greatness, equipped with kingdom strategies, and a willing vessel to be used for Your glory, in Jesus name I pray Amen.

FOLLOW INSTRUCTIONS

Psalm 81
For the director of music. According to gittith. Of Asaph.

1 Sing for joy to God our strength;
   shout aloud to the God of Jacob!
2 Begin the music, strike the timbrel,
   play the melodious harp and lyre.
3 Sound the ram's horn at the New Moon,
   and when the moon is full, on the day of our festival;
4 this is a decree for Israel,
   an ordinance of the God of Jacob.
5 When God went out against Egypt,
   he established it as a statute for Joseph.
   I heard an unknown voice say:
6 "I removed the burden from their shoulders;
   their hands were set free from the basket.
7 In your distress you called and I rescued you,
   I answered you out of a thundercloud;
   I tested you at the waters of Meribah.
8 Hear me, my people, and I will warn you
   if you would only listen to me, Israel!
9 You shall have no foreign god among you;
   you shall not worship any god other than me.
10 I am the Lord your God,
   who brought you up out of Egypt.
  Open wide your mouth and I will fill it.
11 "But my people would not listen to me;
   Israel would not submit to me.
12 So I gave them over to their stubborn hearts
   to follow their own devices.
13 "If my people would only listen to me,
   if Israel would only follow my ways,
14 how quickly I would subdue their enemies
   and turn my hand against their foes!
15 Those who hate the Lord would cringe before him,
   and their punishment would last forever.
16 But you would be fed with the finest of wheat;
   with honey from the rock I would satisfy you."

The nation of Israel was faithful at keeping the laws but resistant from allowing their hearts to truly follow God's provision. Certain times and certain acts of obedience were set aside and done in exact ways of the law. God did things that were sometimes conflicting to the laws put in place and the people didn't quite receive it willingly. This Psalm is dedicated in explaining the importance of allowing God to have full control.

No matter how odd, different, long or short it takes just believe that His commands will come to pass when instructions are willingly followed. Impatience, stubbornness, disbelief and disobedience got the best of them. The Israelites became more comfortable with laws and their own desires rather than the faithfulness of God.

PRAYER

Today Father I learned through your word that says… open my mouth wide and you would fill it with the good things (Psalms 81:10). I realize that I must only speak when spoken through by Your spirit. I must be respectful of the laws of the land, respectful to others, and submissive to authority when it is presented before me. It is better to obey than sacrifice I must be careful to walk in the wisdom of the word every day and honor Your instructions. You know what is best for me and I am not only hearer but a doer of your word (James 1:22). I die to this flesh daily (Luke 9:23) and allow my mind and thoughts to be set on the things of God (Philippians 4:8).

I thank You for the New Covenant of grace that does not keep me in sin, bondage, or death but it separates me into a new life in Christ (Eph. 2:15). I will follow Your instructions (Prov. 3:5-6), in Jesus name I pray Amen.

DO THE RIGHT THING

Psalm 82
A psalm of Asaph.

1 God presides in the great assembly;
    he renders judgment among the "gods":
2 "How long will you defend the unjust
    and show partiality to the wicked?
3 Defend the weak and the fatherless;
    uphold the cause of the poor and the oppressed.
4 Rescue the weak and the needy;
    deliver them from the hand of the wicked.
5 "The 'gods' know nothing, they understand nothing.
    They walk about in darkness;
    all the foundations of the earth are shaken.
6 "I said, 'You are "gods";
    you are all sons of the Most High.'
7 But you will die like mere mortals;
    you will fall like every other ruler."
8 Rise up, O God, judge the earth,
    for all the nations are your inheritance.

Shaking his head in disgust of the injustice actions taking place; Asaph states his case of irritation towards man. People in power miscalculated their position and were filled with pride, hate, and corrupt motives. Asaph demands they put a stop to this charade that does not display the work of a just God. (SN) It's funny as I write this it happens to be the Florida presidential primary results.

Asaph pens a gutsy but truthful message to those reaffirming God's final judgment rest in all people, places, and things. We must humble ourselves in the truth of God's word and not be a people pleaser and depend on the opinions or reactions of man.

PRAYER

Father forgive me of the times when I accepted my increases in life from a natural perspective. Everything that is good and perfect comes from you (Jam. 1:17). You have given me the intellect, capability, skill set, temperament, words, and discernment to be a success for Your glory. Let not my faith be mistaken for pride; nor my confidence be connected with cruelty. I acknowledge You as my Judge and Ruler as You order my steps (Psalm 119:133). In Jesus name I pray Amen.

FIGHT THE ITES

Psalm 83
A song. A psalm of Asaph.

1 O God, do not remain silent;
    do not turn a deaf ear,
    do not stand aloof, O God.
2 See how your enemies growl,
    how your foes rear their heads.
3 With cunning they conspire against your people;
    they plot against those you cherish.
4 "Come," they say, "let us destroy them as a nation,
    so that Israel's name is remembered no more."
5 With one mind they plot together;
    they form an alliance against you
6 the tents of Edom and the Ishmaelites,
    of Moab and the Hagrites,
7 Byblos, Ammon and Amalek,
    Philistia, with the people of Tyre.
8 Even Assyria has joined them
    to reinforce Lot's descendants.
9 Do to them as you did to Midian,
    as you did to Sisera and Jabin at the river Kishon,
10 who perished at Endor
    and became like dung on the ground.
11 Make their nobles like Oreb and Zeeb,
    all their princes like Zebah and Zalmunna,
12 who said, "Let us take possession
    of the pasturelands of God."
13 Make them like tumbleweed, my God,
    like chaff before the wind.
14 As fire consumes the forest
    or a flame sets the mountains ablaze,
15 so pursue them with your tempest
    and terrify them with your storm.
16 Cover their faces with shame, Lord,
    so that they will seek your name.
17 May they ever be ashamed and dismayed;
    may they perish in disgrace.
18 Let them know that you, whose name is the Lord
    that you alone are the Most High over all the earth.

Asaph at the end of his rope with this vicious circle of conspiracy against God and the nation of Israel. His frustration was handled wisely by taking it to God in prayer. He demanded that his prayers be heard in the situation quickly. Everything that had been given to them as an inheritance by God had been eradicated by the Ites (Ites are bad relationships, life snatchers, hateful people). This ploy reminded Asaph to believe God to bring them out from the "ites" as He has done many times before (vs.9-12). Ultimately the end result was to pray that God would have His way and be glorified (vs.13-18).

PRAYER

For though we live in the world we do not wage war as the world does. The weapons we fight with are not the weapons of the world on the contrary they have divine power to demolish strongholds. We demolish arguments and every pretension that sets itself up against the knowledge of God and we take captive every thought to make it obedient to Christ (2 Corinth. 10:3-5). I will fight my "ites" with the strength and power of Your word from:

Bitterness	Jealousy	Fear
Barrenness	Stress	Sickness
Laziness	Doubt	Unhealthy motions
Baggage	Stuck mindset	Limited movement
Limited growth	Time	Being unappreciated
Devalued	Taken for granted	Insomnia
Stolen identity	Suicidal thoughts	Restlessness
Bad habits	Pride	Unforgiveness

All these "ites" are now being conquered with the word of God. It is sharper than any two-edged sword (Heb. 4:12). I will handle Your word with care and believe the truth over a lie. I wait for you Lord and put my hope in Your word (Psalm 130:5), it will not return back to You void (Isa. 55:11). The "ites" in my life have fallen down to their feet never to rise again! Hallelujah in Jesus name I pray Amen.

ENTER IN

Psalm 84
For the director of music. According to gittith. Of the Sons of Korah. A psalm.

1 How lovely is your dwelling place,
   Lord Almighty!
2 My soul yearns, even faints,
   for the courts of the Lord;
   my heart and my flesh cry out
   for the living God.
3 Even the sparrow has found a home,
   and the swallow a nest for herself,
   where she may have her young
   a place near your altar,
   Lord Almighty, my King and my God.
4 Blessed are those who dwell in your house;
   they are ever praising you.
5 Blessed are those whose strength is in you,
   whose hearts are set on pilgrimage.
6 As they pass through the Valley of Baka,
   they make it a place of springs;
   the autumn rains also cover it with pools.
7 They go from strength to strength,
   till each appears before God in Zion.
8 Hear my prayer, Lord God Almighty;
   listen to me, God of Jacob.
9 Look on our shield, O God;
   look with favor on your anointed one.
10 Better is one day in your courts
   than a thousand elsewhere;
   I would rather be a doorkeeper in the house of my God
   than dwell in the tents of the wicked.
11 For the Lord God is a sun and shield;
   the Lord bestows favor and honor;
   no good thing does he withhold
   from those whose walk is blameless.
12 Lord Almighty, blessed is the one who trusts in you

What a heartfelt Psalm of worship acknowledged in beautiful

harmony with who God is. This intense desire created from the heart and soul being a place where He dwells blesses the writer and the reader. Penned by the sons of Korah (worship leaders) it is the words of David boasting about how lovely and satisfying it is to be in God's presence (vs.9). Anyone that is near His presence is looked upon as blessed (vs.3). Through the storms of life, tears and pain, weakness and burdens; God still offers strength and springs of blessings as a place of peace in His everlasting presence. This prayer captures the attention and the essence of worship no matter who we are; but mainly to those who put their trust in Him. No physical place that is adorned as amazing as the deep ocean floor can be as beautiful as being in the presence of the living God.

PRAYER

I enter in Your presence as a true worshiper. Align my heart and spirit with Yours as the two become one. Better is one day in Your courts than a thousand elsewhere I would rather be a doorkeeper in the house of my God then to dwell in the tents of the wicked. For the Lord God is a sun and shield the Lord bestows favor and honor no good thing does he withhold from those who walk is blameless O Lord Almighty Blessed is the man who trust in you (vs.10-12). Hold me close Oh God I know You will never let me go. Only in your presence is there fullness of joy (Psalm 16:11). This joy will not be hijacked by people, nor will my strength be sapped by situations, and my peace will not be pierced by problems. I rejoice in the presence of the Lord that lives on the inside of me (Psalm 139:7), in Jesus name I pray Amen.

I GIVE IN

Psalm 85
For the director of music. Of the Sons of Korah. A psalm.

1 You, Lord, showed favor to your land;
    you restored the fortunes of Jacob.
2 You forgave the iniquity of your people
    and covered all their sins.
3 You set aside all your wrath
    and turned from your fierce anger.
4 Restore us again, God our Savior,
    and put away your displeasure toward us.
5 Will you be angry with us forever?
    Will you prolong your anger through all generations?
6 Will you not revive us again,
    that your people may rejoice in you?
7 Show us your unfailing love, Lord,
    and grant us your salvation.
8 I will listen to what God the Lord says;
    he promises peace to his people, his faithful servants
    but let them not turn to folly.
9 Surely his salvation is near those who fear him,
    that his glory may dwell in our land.
10 Love and faithfulness meet together;
    righteousness and peace kiss each other.
11 Faithfulness springs forth from the earth,
    and righteousness looks down from heaven.
12 The Lord will indeed give what is good,
    and our land will yield its harvest.
13 Righteousness goes before him
    and prepares the way for his steps.

Demotion as a nation was at its worse. Overwhelming evidence of a deserted presence of God enhanced the very fact of their need for Him. They needed Him now more than ever before and the mission became priority. Giving into the sweet salvation of God's promises initiates hope, peace, righteousness, and love.

Salvation from God was like kissing the face of destiny and that is what the people longed for. Giving in was not an act of weakness but it was an act of surrender to be fully used for His glory.

PRAYER

As David said in Psalm 51:11… Do not cast me away from your presence or take your Holy Spirit from me. You are what I need to survive in this life. I now understand the importance of salvation and where it positions me as a child of God. Your salvation prepares me to:

- Stand in hope when I am weary and depleted
- Peace when I am confused and unsettled
- Righteousness when I am accused and disrespected
- Love when I am rejected and alone

Salvation grants me forgiveness of my sins and leads me to God's glory. I give into not what it looks or feels like but I give into the rest of God's salvation for my life. In Jesus name I pray Amen.

SOUL FOOD

Psalm 86
A prayer of David.

1 Hear me, Lord, and answer me,
    for I am poor and needy.
2 Guard my life, for I am faithful to you;
    save your servant who trusts in you.
    You are my God; 3 have mercy on me, Lord,
    for I call to you all day long.
4 Bring joy to your servant, Lord,
    for I put my trust in you.
5 You, Lord, are forgiving and good,
    abounding in love to all who call to you.
6 Hear my prayer, Lord;
    listen to my cry for mercy.
7 When I am in distress, I call to you,
    because you answer me.
8 Among the gods there is none like you, Lord;
    no deeds can compare with yours.
9 All the nations you have made
    will come and worship before you, Lord;
    they will bring glory to your name.
10 For you are great and do marvelous deeds;
    you alone are God.
11 Teach me your way, Lord,
    that I may rely on your faithfulness;
    give me an undivided heart,
    that I may fear your name.
12 I will praise you, Lord my God, with all my heart;
    I will glorify your name forever.
13 For great is your love toward me;
    you have delivered me from the depths,
    from the realm of the dead.
14 Arrogant foes are attacking me, O God;
    ruthless people are trying to kill me
    they have no regard for you.
15 But you, Lord, are a compassionate and gracious God,
    slow to anger, abounding in love and faithfulness.
16 Turn to me and have mercy on me;
    show your strength in behalf of your servant;
    save me, because I serve you

just as my mother did.
17 Give me a sign of your goodness,
    that my enemies may see it and be put to shame,
    for you, Lord, have helped me and comforted me.

Never resistant but always ready is the very character of God's heart towards us. David's prayer was only to be heard by the ear of God directly deep from David's soul. His expression of the outward appearance as being always needy and weak; but inwardly being comforted in abundance revealed what is truly important for the life of the believer. His prayers pleaded with a yearning need for God's mercy and love to devour his soul. Physically David was incompetent to think clearly and dissatisfied with life. He was hungry spiritually to be a glory carrier of God's unmatched truth, dedicated love, and abounding faithfulness. The mere fact that David's life was in the state of decline his soul cried out to be fed by the living proof of God's truth.

Pray Psalm 86

SPIRITUAL CITIZENSHIP

Psalm 87
Of the Sons of Korah. A psalm. A song.

1 He has founded his city on the holy mountain.
2 The Lord loves the gates of Zion
   more than all the other dwellings of Jacob.
3 Glorious things are said of you,
   city of God:
4 "I will record Rahab and Babylon
   among those who acknowledge me
   Philistia too, and Tyre, along with Cush
   and will say, 'This one was born in Zion.'"
5 Indeed, of Zion it will be said,
   "This one and that one were born in her,
   and the Most High himself will establish her."
6 The Lord will write in the register of the peoples:
   "This one was born in Zion."
7 As they make music they will sing,
   "All my fountains are in you."

Zion is known as a place that God loves. A fortress was built around Zion high up on a mountain by David as of monument of protection for God's people. Zion in this day was referred to as a "her". This is metaphoric word known as to where you can go to get nurtured, established in the law, and loved by God. In Zion no necessary paperwork needs to be filled out. Zion was simply a place where God's presence was known and acknowledged. Now as a New Testament covenant we no longer have to physically go to a place every day to encounter His presence. Although we should have a place of worship to fellowship; God's presence lives on the inside of every believer. As they sang and made music in Zion so should we every day as a believer.

PRAYER

Dear Father make this earthly tent (body) as Zion the place where you dwell. Make the foundation of my heart be a place where Your love dwells and is felt. Make my spirit one with Your Holy Spirit that will fashion me to be more like You. Make my mouth to speak praise of the One and Only True Living God who lives on the inside of me. Today I am born again as a citizen of the kingdom of God. I am seated in heavenly places (Eph. 2:6), an incorruptible seed (1 Pet. 1:23) as a child of the Most High God. You qualify me and establish me and I will forever acknowledge You as my Savior Hallelujah! In Jesus name I pray Amen.

DONNA ROBINSON

DEPRESSION OVERLOAD

Psalm 88
A song. A psalm of the Sons of Korah. For the director of music.
According to mahalath leannoth. A maskil of Heman the Ezrahite.

1 Lord, you are the God who saves me;
    day and night I cry out to you.
2 May my prayer come before you;
    turn your ear to my cry.
3 I am overwhelmed with troubles
    and my life draws near to death.
4 I am counted among those who go down to the pit;
    I am like one without strength.
5 I am set apart with the dead,
    like the slain who lie in the grave,
  whom you remember no more,
    who are cut off from your care.
6 You have put me in the lowest pit,
    in the darkest depths.
7 Your wrath lies heavily on me;
    you have overwhelmed me with all your waves.
8 You have taken from me my closest friends
    and have made me repulsive to them.
    I am confined and cannot escape;
9 my eyes are dim with grief.
    I call to you, Lord, every day;
    I spread out my hands to you.
10 Do you show your wonders to the dead?
    Do their spirits rise up and praise you?
11 Is your love declared in the grave,
    your faithfulness in Destruction?
12 Are your wonders known in the place of darkness,
    or your righteous deeds in the land of oblivion?
13 But I cry to you for help, Lord;
    in the morning my prayer comes before you.
14 Why, Lord, do you reject me
    and hide your face from me?
15 From my youth I have suffered and been close to death;
    I have borne your terrors and am in despair.
16 Your wrath has swept over me;
    your terrors have destroyed me.
17 All day long they surround me like a flood;

they have completely engulfed me.
18 You have taken from me friend and neighbor
darkness is my closest friend.

The author of this Psalm is Heman (name means faithful). A songwriter who expresses how he was stricken with deep depression. Unknown to pinpoint if this was in reference to past mistreatment from people, or if it was present tragedies from manipulated relationships. It is evident of the pain Heman is now feeling. Although he gives much attention to the pain he still does the right thing and gives it all to God in prayer. Alive in the flesh but feeling dead in spirit overwhelmed him to the point of accepting darkness as his closest friend (vs.18). God is so amazing still; He blessed Heman with such wisdom and strength to bear this cross and he handles it like a Christian should with nonstop prayer. Prayer as his first point of action from morning to night and day to day. God knew what Heman could handle and while in the state of depression, despair, and destruction he kept his faith in God that his prayers will soon be answered.

PRAYER

Father you are my Guiding Light when I cannot see where my life is headed. My salvation in You does not exempt me from pain, problems, or persecution. Whatever I'm going through right now I give it all over to You in prayer and I ask You receive me and turn Your ear to me as I cry out to You.

Prayer changes things but most importantly it changes me! Prayer will always be my first line of defense and will position me for power.

- When I am in trouble I will pray.
- When I am overwhelmed I will pray
- When I am confused I will pray
- When I am impatient I will pray
- When I am sick I will pray
- When I am moody I will pray
- When I am tired I will pray
- When I am under emotional attack I will pray

I will be joyful in hope, patient in affliction, and faithful in prayer (Rom. 12:12) in Jesus name I pray Amen.

WITNESSES OF GOD'S COVENANT

Psalm 89
A maskil of Ethan the Ezrahite.

1 I will sing of the Lord's great love forever;
  with my mouth I will make your faithfulness known
  through all generations.
2 I will declare that your love stands firm forever,
  that you have established your faithfulness in heaven itself.
3 You said, "I have made a covenant with my chosen one,
  I have sworn to David my servant,
4 'I will establish your line forever
  and make your throne firm through all generations.'"
5 The heavens praise your wonders, Lord,
  your faithfulness too, in the assembly of the holy ones.
6 For who in the skies above can compare with the Lord?
  Who is like the Lord among the heavenly beings?
7 In the council of the holy ones God is greatly feared;
  he is more awesome than all who surround him.
8 Who is like you, Lord God Almighty?
  You, Lord, are mighty, and your faithfulness surrounds you.
9 You rule over the surging sea;
  when its waves mount up, you still them.
10 You crushed Rahab like one of the slain;
  with your strong arm you scattered your enemies.
11 The heavens are yours, and yours also the earth;
  you founded the world and all that is in it.
12 You created the north and the south;
  Tabor and Hermon sing for joy at your name.
13 Your arm is endowed with power;
  your hand is strong, your right hand exalted.
14 Righteousness and justice are the foundation of your throne;
  love and faithfulness go before you.
15 Blessed are those who have learned to acclaim you,
  who walk in the light of your presence, Lord.
16 They rejoice in your name all day long;
  they celebrate your righteousness.
17 For you are their glory and strength,
  and by your favor you exalt our horn.
18 Indeed, our shield belongs to the Lord,
  our king to the Holy One of Israel.
19 Once you spoke in a vision,

to your faithful people you said:
  "I have bestowed strength on a warrior;
  I have raised up a young man from among the people.
20 I have found David my servant;
  with my sacred oil I have anointed him.
21 My hand will sustain him;
  surely my arm will strengthen him.
22 The enemy will not get the better of him;
  the wicked will not oppress him.
23 I will crush his foes before him
  and strike down his adversaries.
24 My faithful love will be with him,
  and through my name his horn will be exalted.
25 I will set his hand over the sea,
  his right hand over the rivers.
26 He will call out to me, 'You are my Father,
  my God, the Rock my Savior.'
27 And I will appoint him to be my firstborn,
  the most exalted of the kings of the earth.
28 I will maintain my love to him forever,
  and my covenant with him will never fail.
29 I will establish his line forever,
  his throne as long as the heavens endure.
30 "If his sons forsake my law
  and do not follow my statutes,
31 if they violate my decrees
  and fail to keep my commands,
32 I will punish their sin with the rod,
  their iniquity with flogging;
33 but I will not take my love from him,
  nor will I ever betray my faithfulness.
34 I will not violate my covenant
  or alter what my lips have uttered.
35 Once for all, I have sworn by my holiness
  and I will not lie to David
36 that his line will continue forever
  and his throne endure before me like the sun;
37 it will be established forever like the moon,
  the faithful witness in the sky."
38 But you have rejected, you have spurned,
  you have been very angry with your anointed one.
39 You have renounced the covenant with your servant
  and have defiled his crown in the dust.

40 You have broken through all his walls
   and reduced his strongholds to ruins.
41 All who pass by have plundered him;
   he has become the scorn of his neighbors.
42 You have exalted the right hand of his foes;
   you have made all his enemies rejoice.
43 Indeed, you have turned back the edge of his sword
   and have not supported him in battle.
44 You have put an end to his splendor
   and cast his throne to the ground.
45 You have cut short the days of his youth;
   you have covered him with a mantle of shame.
46 How long, Lord? Will you hide yourself forever?
   How long will your wrath burn like fire?
47 Remember how fleeting is my life.
   For what futility you have created all humanity!
48 Who can live and not see death,
   or who can escape the power of the grave?
49 Lord, where is your former great love,
   which in your faithfulness you swore to David?
50 Remember, Lord, how your servant has been mocked,
   how I bear in my heart the taunts of all the nations,
51 the taunts with which your enemies, Lord, have mocked,
   with which they have mocked every step of your anointed one.
52 Praise be to the Lord forever!
   Amen and Amen.

Penning this Psalm speaks of our rightful place in God's covenant for every believer. Ethan (name means strong) was a very wise man (1 Kings 4:31) who poured out his heart about his love for God. Ethan recognized this devoted commitment from the Lord. He spoke of how nature from the skies to the seas are witnesses of this covenant. He spoke of the Davidic covenant (God's promises) and how He established David to be a kingly witness of this covenant. He even spoke of the New Testament covenant of Jesus whom we all are witnesses of this covenant today Hallelujah! He then pronounces the consequences of forsaking the covenant and God's amazing faithfulness of love even when betrayed (vs.30-34). Ultimately our choices will define how true we are to the covenant whether the consequences are good or bad.

PRAYER

Lord as long as I have breath in my body I stand as a firm believer of Your indestructible covenant for all mankind to witness here on earth. I understand the choices I make today effects the outcomes of my tomorrow. My prayer is I stay close to Your covenant purposed plan in every decision I make. I choose to be a witness of worship and rejoice in Your name all day long. I choose to be a witness of praise as Your faithfulness surrounds me. I choose to stay committed to the character of God as a witness to a dying world. Thank you Jesus for Your New Testament covenant that allows every single human being to be free from the penalty of sin. This covenant establishes me to walk in the light of Your presence in Jesus name I pray Amen.

TERMS/REFERENCES:

- Maskil: understanding, learned, enlightened, to teach
- Miktam: technical term found in Psalm titles

BACKGROUND

- Sons of Korah: lineage of Levites responsible for the music and songs of the temple
- Asaph: seer, worship leader (1 Chronicles 25)
- Heman: Levite, writer of songs and poems, seer (1 Chronicles 25
- Ethan: wise man of God (1 Kings 4:31)
- Israelites: God's chosen people of the Old testament covenant

REFERENCES:

All scriptures are taken from www.biblegateway.com

NIV version

ABOUT THE AUTHOR

Donna Robinson is a woman of God who possesses a heart of a worshipper. She stands alongside her husband and fully supports him and the vision of New Day Christian Center in Apopka, FL. God has placed unique gifts of discernment, intercession, encourager, and strong leadership qualities in her that will enhance the body of Christ. Native born Floridian she enjoys traveling, music, and lots of shopping! She is a graduate of Valencia Community College with an Associate's Degree in Office Administration and has also obtained her Bachelor's Degree from Barry University in Business Administration with at Specialization in Human Resources. As a mother, wife, friend, and sister she strives to live life as a servant of God.